-British-
WARSHIPS
Since 1945

by Mike Critchley

(Part 1)

HMS Rodney

£1.80

As a result of the highly successful annual reference book 'British Warships & Auxiliaries' (which covers the modern fleet) I have been asked to produce this little book to record the ships of the Royal Navy *since* World War II.

Many of the ships in the following pages had distinguished careers during the War — but their exploits are well recorded elsewhere. The post war era — as far as I know — has not been previously covered. As much information as possible is included although those who served in these ships at the time will doubtless point out 'glaring omissions' — I apologise!

Details of the ships are given as they appeared in 1945 — many were reconstructed during the war when various items of equipment and armaments were added — or removed.

I have deliberately omitted the large number of ships that were scrapped as soon as hostilities ceased.

Finally, without the help of Lieut. Cdr. Ken Burns, DSM., RN. (Rtd.), former Naval Historian at Plymouth Central Library, this book could not have been produced — I am indeed grateful for his help.

I trust you enjoy the end result.

Mike Critchley

Looe, Cornwall

2

By Admiral Sir Guy Grantham,
KCB, CBE, DSO,
Commander in Chief Mediterranean
1954-1957
Commander in Chief Portsmouth
1957-1959

At sea during the 1950's when I was a Senior Officer Afloat, the Fleet mainly consisted of ships built towards the end of World War II — or shortly afterwards. Many had played an important part in war operations.

Vanguard was the only battleship, Eagle and Ark Royal were the two largest aircraft carriers and there were also the large ships of the Hermes and Colossus classes — and a considerable number of Cruisers, Destroyers and smaller vessels. Nuclear submarines, now carrying battleship names because of their importance, were not in commission, and the fleet as a whole could be classed as 'conventional'. There were no ships armed with missiles.

The gun and carrier-borne aircraft were the weapons of attack — and ships' crews were correspondingly numerous.

Routine was much the same as in pre-war days, and most of the customary overseas stations and commands had been re-established. Ships were still commanded, and operated, from the bridge. Operations rooms were gradually developing but were a shadow of what has since evolved. However they proved their real effectiveness in the Korean and Suez operations.

There were no lack of tasks for the Fleet and the presence of HM Ships undoubtedly had a sobering effect in world trouble spots — and they were also able to give great help in areas where floods, fires and earthquakes caused disruption. All the skills, equipment and stores carried in ships were in frequent use in many parts of the world where people's lives were disrupted by hurricanes and other disasters.

Perhaps the greatest difference between the Navy of the fifties and modern times was the longer commissions ships carried out — and the availability of overseas bases — which have now almost disappeared. Officers and men serving abroad were able to have their families with them in Gibraltar, Malta, Aden, Singapore, Hong Kong, Bermuda, Simonstown and several other places. The opportunity for families to travel and live overseas made for contentment and the pressure on personnel to leave the Service was far less than today. The provision of married quarters has not altogether proved to be a substitute.

The 50's were happy days and we all enjoyed a life which is no longer available, serving in ships which were well found and suitable for their tasks — even if living conditions were austere by modern standards.

I feel fortunate to have served afloat during the period covered by this book.

Guy Grantham

Liss, Hampshire

3

Battleships

NELSON CLASS

Ship	Launch Date	Builder
NELSON	3 Sept. 1925	Armstrong Whitworth Ltd., Newcastle
RODNEY	17 Dec. 1925	Cammell Laird, Birkenhead

Displacement 33,950 tons (Rodney 33,900 tons) **Length** 710 ft. **Beam** 106 ft. **Draught** 28 ft. 6 ins. **Speed** 23 knots **Armament** nine 16″, twelve 6″, six 4.7″ (Nelson only), eight 4″ (Rodney only), sixteen 40mm AA, forty-eight 2 PDR AA, sixty-one 20mm AA **Aircraft** one **Torpedo Tubes** two 24.5″ (submerged) **Complement** 1,314.

Notes

First ships to mount 16″ guns.

NELSON
1946 Flagship of Rear Admiral Training Battleships.
1948/9 Used as a bombing targeet.
15 March 1949 Arrived Inverkeithing for breaking up.

RODNEY (Photo Page 1)
No effective Post-war role.
26 March 1948 Arrived Inverkeithing for breaking up.

HMS Nelson (March 1946)

Battleships

KING GEORGE V CLASS

Ship	Launch Date	Builder
KING GEORGE V	21 Feb 1939	Vickers Armstrong Ltd, Tyne
DUKE OF YORK (Ex-Anson)	28 Feb 1940	John Brown & Co., Ltd. - Clydebank
ANSON (Ex-Jellicoe)	24 Feb 1940	Swan Hunter & Wigham Richardson, Wallsend
HOWE (Ex-Beatty)	9 April 1940	Fairfield Shipbuilding & Eng. Co., Ltd, Govan

Displacement 35,000 tons **Length** 745 ft. **Beam** 103 ft. **Draught** 27ft. 8 ins. **Speed** 29 knots **Armament** ten 14", sixteen 5.25", c. sixty 2 PDR AA, up to fourteen each 40mm AA and 20mm AA, and four 3 PDR. (Numbers of smaller weapons varied in each ship) **Complement** 1,553 - 1,613.

Notes

KING GEORGE V

1946	—	Flagship of Commander-in-Chief, Home Fleet.
1947-50	—	Home Fleet.
14 June 1950	—	Laid up in the Gareloch.
20 Jan. 1958	—	Towed to Dalmuir for breaking up. (The hull at Troon)

HMS King George V (August 1946)

HMS Duke of York (January 1947)

Battleships

Notes

DUKE OF YORK

After VE-Day	—	Sailed for Japan. Was Flagship of Admiral Fraser in Tokyo for surrender of Japan.
July 1946	—	Returned to Plymouth.
1947-49	—	Flagship of Commander-in-Chief, Home Fleet, before being placed in reserve in 1949.
1950-51	—	Flag Officer Commanding Reserve Fleet.
From Sept. 1951	—	Laid up in the Gareloch.
Feb. 1958	—	Broken up at Faslane.

ANSON

Aug. 1945	—	Occupation of Hong Kong and afterwards Guardship at Tokyo.
Jan. 1946	—	To Australia.
July 1946	—	Arrived Portsmouth.
1948-49	—	Flag Officer, Training Squadron.
1950	—	In reserve in the Gareloch.
17 Dec. 1957	—	Arrived Faslane for breaking up.

HOWE

Jan. 1946	—	Arrived Portsmouth and became Training Ship.
1947	—	Flag Officer, Training Battleships.
1950	—	HQ Ship — Senior Officer Reserve Fleet, Portsmouth.
1952	—	In Reserve.
2 June 1958	—	Arrived Inverkeithing for breaking up.

A fifth ship, HMS Prince of Wales, built by Cammell Laird & Co., was lost in December, 1941.

Note: The first battleships to have 14″ guns and in quadruple mountings.

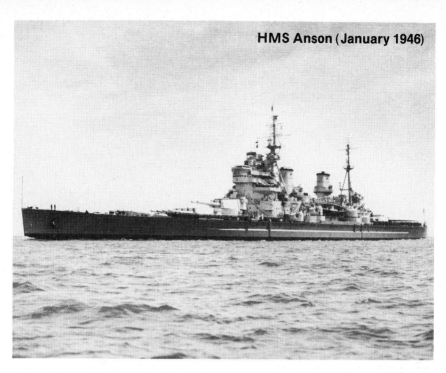

HMS Anson (January 1946)

HMS Howe (March 1946)

Battleships

VANGUARD CLASS

Ship	Launch Date	Builder
VANGUARD	30 Nov. 1944	John Brown & Co., Ltd., Clydebank

Displacement 44,500 tons **Length** 814 ft. 4 ins. **Beam** 108 ft. 6 ins. **Draught** 28 ft. **Speed** 30 knots **Armament** eight 15″, sixteen 5.25″, fifty-eight 40mm AA, four 3 PDR **Complement** 1,600 (peace).

Notes

15″ guns were first mounted in ''COURAGEOUS'' and ''GLORIOUS'' in 1917.

Feb.-May 1947	—	Royal Tour to South Africa.
1947-48	—	Refitted at Devonport.
Jan.-July 1949	—	In Mediterranean.
Nov. 1949	—	Training Ship at Portland.
1950-51	—	Wore Flag of C-in-C., Home Fleet.
May 1951	—	Flagship of Training Squadron.
Sept. 1951	—	To refit.
1952-1954	—	Flagship of Home Fleet.
1954-55	—	To refit (at Devonport) — thence to Flagship of Reserve Fleet & NATO Headquarters ship at Portsmouth.
7 June 1960	—	De-commissioned.
4 Aug. 1960	—	Ran aground during tow from Portsmouth to breaker's yard. Pulled clear by 8 tugs.
9 Aug. 1960	—	Arrived at Faslane for breaking up.

HMS Vanguard (May 1953)

Fleet Aircraft Carriers

ILLUSTRIOUS CLASS

Ship	Launch Date	Builder
ILLUSTRIOUS	5 April 1939	Vickers Armstrong Ltd., Barrow-in-Furness
FORMIDABLE	17 Aug. 1939	Harland & Wolff Ltd., Belfast
VICTORIOUS	14 Sept. 1939	Vickers Armstrong Ltd. Tyne

Displacement 23,000 tons (increased after reconstruction in 1958) **Length** 753 ft. **Beam** 95 ft. **Draught** 24 ft. **Speed** 31 knots **Armament** sixteen 4.5", forty 2 PDR AA, three 40mm AA, fifty-two 20mm AA **Aircraft** over 60 **Complement** 1,600.

Notes

FORMIDABLE

1945	—	Pacific Fleet.
1948	—	Into Reserve Fleet.
7 May 1953	—	Towed from Portsmouth for breaking up at Inverkeithing.

HMS Formidable (February 1946)

Fleet Aircraft Carriers

Notes

ILLUSTRIOUS

27 June 1945	—	Arrived in the Forth for four month refit, but was delayed until June 1946. Operated in Home waters until end of 1947 carrying out trials as a deck-landing ship.
1948	—	Refitted and considerably modernised before returning to sea duties in September.
1948-54	—	Trials and Training Carrier in Home Waters.
1951	—	Used to carry troops to Cyprus.
1954	—	Laid up in the Gareloch before being approved for disposal on 11 October 1956.
3 Nov. 1956	—	Arrived Faslane for breaking up.

HMS Illustrious (July 1946)

Fleet Aircraft Carriers

Notes

VICTORIOUS

1945	—	Pacific Fleet.
1950-58	—	Reconstructed at Portsmouth when her length was increased by 30 ft; her beam 7ft. 8 ins.; and her draught by 1 ft. 9 ins.
1959	—	Visited U.S.A. to demonstrate her advanced type 984 radar.
May 1962-Aug 1963	—	Refitted at Portsmouth
July 1966	—	Sailed for Far East.
21 June 1967	—	Arrived Portsmouth.
Nov. 1967	—	Serious fire on board in Portsmouth as a result of which it was decided not to repair and recommission her.
July 1969	—	Sold.
July 1970	—	Arrived Faslane for breaking up.

HMS Victorious (October 1945)

16

Fleet Aircraft Carriers

MODIFIED ILLUSTRIOUS CLASS

Ship	Launch Date	Builder
INDOMITABLE	26 March 1940	Vickers Armstrong Ltd. Barrow-in-Furness

Displacement 23,500 tons **Length** 759 ft. 8 ins **Beam** 95 ft. 9 ins. **Draught** 24 ft. **Speed** 30.5 knots **Armament** sixteen 4.5″ twenty-four 40mm AA, forty 2 PDR AA, four 3 PDR **Aircraft** 65 **Complement** 1,600.

Notes

INDOMITABLE

1945	—	Pacific Fleet.
1948-50	—	Extensive refit and modernisation when bow and stern were re-built.
1951-52	—	Flagship of Commander-in-Chief, Home Fleet.
1954	—	In Reserve.
30 Sept. 1955	—	Arrived Faslane for breaking up.

HMS Indomitable (June 1953)

Fleet Aircraft Carriers

IMPLACABLE CLASS

Ship	Launch Date	Builder
IMPLACABLE	10 Dec. 1942	Fairfield Shipbuilding & Eng. Co., Ltd. Govan
INDEFATIGABLE	8 Dec. 1942	John Brown & co., Ltd. Clydebank

Displacement 26,000 tons **Length** 766 ft. 5 ins. **Beam** 131 ft. 3 ins. **Draught** 29 ft. 9 ins. **Speed** 32.5 knots **Armament** sixteen 4.5″, twelve 40mm AA, nine 20mm AA, fifty-two 2 PDR AA, four 3 PDR **Aircraft** 72 **Complement** 1,785.

Notes

IMPLACABLE

1945	—	Pacific Fleet.
1948-49	—	Refit.
1949-50	—	Flagship of Commander-in-Chief, Home Fleet.
1951	—	Training Squadron.
1954	—	Reduced to Reserve.
3 Nov. 1955	—	Arrived Inverkeithing for breaking up.

HMS Implacable (May 1949)

Fleet Aircraft Carriers

Notes

INDEFATIGABLE

1945	—	Pacific Fleet.
1948	—	Reserve Fleet.
1949	—	Taken out of Reserve.
1950	—	Refitted at Devonport for Training Squadron.
1951	—	Flagship of the Training Squadron.
1954	—	Again reduced to Reserve.
4 Nov. 1956	—	Arrived Dalmuir for breaking up.

HMS Indefatigable (June 1953)

Light Fleet Aircraft Carriers

COLOSSUS CLASS

Ship	Launch Date	Builder
COLOSSUS	30 Sept. 1943	Vickers Armstrong Ltd., Tyne
GLORY	27 Nov. 1943	Harland & Wolff Ltd., Belfast
VENERABLE	30 Dec. 1943	Cammell Laird & Co. Ltd., Birkenhead
VENGEANCE	23 Feb. 1944	Swan Hunter & Wigham Richardson Ltd., Wallsend
WARRIOR	20 May 1944	Harland & Wolff Ltd., Belfast
THESEUS	6 July 1944	Fairfield Shipbuilding & Eng. Co. Ltd., Govan
OCEAN	8 July 1944	Alex Stephen & Sons Ltd., Govan
TRIUMPH	2 Oct. 1944	R & W Hawthorn Leslie & Co. Ltd., Hebburn

Displacement 13,190 tons (Theseus, Triumph & Warrior 13,350 tons) **Length** 695 ft. **Beam** 112 ft. 6 ins. across the Flight Deck **Draught** 21 ft. 4 ins. **Speed** 25 knots **Armament** four 3 PDR, twenty-four 2 PDR AA, nineteen 40mm AA (see note) **Aircraft** 39-44 **Complement** c. 850 (excluding Squadron personnel).

Note: Number of guns varied in each ship. GLORY 29 - 40mm; OCEAN 30 - 40mm; THESEUS and TRIUMPH as above; VENGEANCE 12 - 40mm and 32 - 20mm; WARRIOR 28 - 40mm; 2-3 PDR.

HMS Glory (October 1939)

Light Fleet Aircraft Carriers

Notes

GLORY

1945	—	Pacific Fleet. Made three trips conveying prisoners of war back to Australia.
1947	—	Returned from Far East, to remain in Reserve until Nov. 1949.
Dec. 1950	—	Re-commissioned.
1951-53	—	Korean War, interspersed with a refit in Australia and a visit to the Mediterranean.
1954	—	Trooping and Ferry Carrier.
1956-61	—	In Reserve at Rosyth.
Aug. 1961	—	Arrived at Inverkeithing for breaking up.

COLOSSUS

6 Aug. 1946	—	Lent to French Navy for five years with option to purchase.
1951	—	Sold to France and re-named ARROMANCHES.
1957-58	—	Refitted, and employed as Training Carrier, without guns.
1974	—	Disposal List.
1978	—	Broken up at Toulon.

VENGEANCE

1950-51	—	Flagship of Third Aircraft Carrier Squadron.
13 Nov. 1952	—	Handed over at Devonport to the Royal Australian Navy.
1953-55	—	Loaned to R.A.N.
12 Aug. 1955	—	Arrived back at Devonport where her crew took over the "MELBOURNE".
14. Dec. 1956	—	Sold to Brazil.
1957-60	—	Reconstructed at Rotterdam where she commissioned on 6 Dec. 1960.
13 Jan. 1961	—	Left Rotterdam under her new name "MINAS GERAIS".

HMS Vengeance (August 1947)

Light Fleet Aircraft Carriers

Notes

WARRIOR

1946-48	—	Lent to Royal Canadian Navy.
1952-53	—	Modernised.
1955-56	—	Again Modernised.
Feb.-Oct. 1957	—	Headquarters ship of atomic tests in Christmas Island.
July 1958	—	Sold to Argentina.
10 Dec. 1958	—	Left Portsmouth.
26 Jan. 1959	—	Commissioned under new name "INDEPENDENCIA" at Puerto Belgrano Naval Base.
1971	—	Disposal List.

TRIUMPH

1945	—	Pacific Fleet.
1947	—	Flagship of Flag Officer (Air) in Mediterranean.
1948	—	F.O. (Air) Mediterranean and Second-in-Command, Mediterranean Fleet.
1953	—	Accommodation modified for Officer Cadets Training Ship.
1958-1965	—	Converted to Heavy Repair Ship at Portsmouth. Relieved "Hartland Point" in Singapore as Escort Maintenance Ship.
1972	—	Returned to U.K. to pay off.
1975	—	In Reserve at Chatham.
1980	—	For disposal.

HMS Warrior (October 1948)

HMS Triumph (July 1951)

Light Fleet Aircraft Carriers

Notes

THESEUS

1947	—	Flagship of Flag Officer (Air) in Far East.
1948-49	—	Flagship of 3rd Aircraft Carrier Squadron.
1951-52	—	Korean War.
1952	—	Flagship of Flag Officer, Heavy Squadron, Home Fleet and Flag Officer Commanding 2nd Aircraft Carrier Squadron.
1954	—	Refitted for Training Squadron Role.
1955-56	—	Flagship of Flag Officer, Training Squadron, Home Fleet.
1958	—	In Reserve.
29 May 1962	—	Arrived Inverkeithing for breaking up.

OCEAN (Photo — outside back cover)

1949	—	Flagship of Flag Officer (Air) and Second-in-Command, Mediterranean Fleet.
1952	—	Korean War.
1954	—	Refitted for Training Squadron Rôle.
1957	—	Flagship of Flag Officer, Training Squadron, Home Fleet.
1958	—	In Reserve.
6 May 1962	—	Arrived Faslane for breaking up.

VENERABLE

1 April 1948	—	Sold to Royal Netherlands Navy, re-named Karel Doorman and commissioned 28 May 1948.
1955-58	—	Modernisation.
29 April 1968	—	Damaged by boiler fire.
15 Oct. 1968	—	Sold to Argentina, refitted at Rotterdam.
12 March 1969	—	Commissioned into the Argentine Navy as "VEINTICINCO DE MAYO".

HMS Theseus (April 1953)

Light Fleet Aircraft Carriers

MAJESTIC CLASS

Ship	Launch Date	Builder
TERRIBLE	30 Sept. 1944	Devonport Dockyard
MAGNIFICENT	16 Nov. 1944	Harland & Wolff Ltd., Belfast
POWERFUL	27 Feb. 1945	Harland & Wolff Ltd., Belfast
MAJESTIC	28 Feb. 1945	Vickers & Armstrong Ltd., Barrow-in-Furness
LEVIATHAN	7 June 1945	Swan Hunter & Wigham Richardson, Wallsend
HERCULES	22 Sept. 1945	Vickers Armstrong Ltd., Tyne

Displacement 14,000 tons **Length** 695 ft. **Beam** 112 ft. 6 ins. across Flight Deck **Draught** 21 ft. 4 ins. **Speed** 25 knots **Armament** four 3 PDR, thirty 40mm AA **Aircraft** 39 to 44 **Complement** c. 850 (Excluding Squadron personnel).

Notes

TERRIBLE

	—	Only Aircraft Carrier ever built in a Royal Dockyard.
16 Dec. 1948	—	Handed over to Royal Australian Navy and re-named "SYDNEY".
1951-52	—	Korean War.
1955-58	—	Training Ship.
1961-62	—	Converted to Fast Troop Transport Vessel.
1962	—	Vietnam War.
1973	—	Paid off into Reserve.
23 Dec. 1975	—	Towed from Sydney to be broken up in South Korea by Dong Kuk Steel Mill Co., Ltd.

HMS Terrible (as HMAS Sydney Feb 1949)

Light Fleet Aircraft Carriers

Notes

MAGNIFICENT

| | | Lent to the Royal Canadian Navy. |
| 12 July 1965 | — | Arrived Faslane for breaking up. |

POWERFUL

May 1946	—	Construction suspended.
July 1952	—	Work resumed when ship was purchased by Canada and re-named "BONAVENTURE".
1 April 1970	—	Paid off.
		Sold for breaking up, to M.W. Kennedy Ltd., Vancouver B.C. and towed to Taiwan from Halifax on 27 Oct. 1970.

LEVIATHAN

May 1946	—	When structurally almost complete, work stopped.
July 1946	—	Towed to Portsmouth. Used as spare parts for refit of HMNLS KAREL DOORMAN when sold to Argentina.
27 May 1968	—	Arrived Faslane for breaking up.

HMS Powerful (as HMCS Bonaventure Oct 1962)

Light Fleet Aircraft Carriers

Notes

MAJESTIC

At the end of the Second World War, work ceased.

1949-55	—	Reconstruction and Modernisation.
28 Oct. 1955	—	Commissioned and re-named MELBOURNE, for the Royal Australian Navy, at Barrow-in-Furness.
14 May 1956	—	Flagship of R.A.N.
1969	—	Extended refit.
Nov.1972-July 1973	—	Refitted.
		Expected to remain in service until 1985.

HERCULES

May 1946	—	Construction stopped.
May 1947	—	Laid up at Faslane.
Jan.1957	—	Sold to India.
April 1957	—	Arrived Belfast for large scale reconstruction and modernisation by Harland & Wolff Ltd.
4 March 1961	—	Renamed VIKRANT and commissioned into R.I.N.

HMS Majestic (as HMAS Melbourne June 1977)

Light Fleet Aircraft Carriers

CENTAUR CLASS

Ship	Launch Date	Builder
CENTAUR	22 April 1947	Harland & Wolff Ltd., Belfast
ALBION	6 May 1947	Swan Hunter & Wigham Richardson Ltd., Wallsend
BULWARK	22 June 1948	Harland & Wolff Ltd., Belfast

Displacement 22,000 tons **Length** 737 ft. 9 ins. **Beam** 123 ft. **Draught** 26 ft. **Speed** 28 knots **Armament** twenty-six 40mm AA, four 3 PDR **Aircraft** 45 **Complement** c. 1,350 (with Squadrons embarked).

Notes

CENTAUR

1954	—	Completed.
1956-58	—	Modernised at Devonport — fitted with steam catapults and new arrester gear.
1961	—	Kuwait.
1964	—	Transported Royal Marines to Tanganyika.
Aug. 1965	—	Took part in Review of the Fleet in the Clyde. Afterwards returned to Portsmouth to act as accommodation ship for VICTORIOUS refitting.
Sept. 1966	—	Towed from Portsmouth to Devonport for use as accommodation ship for "EAGLE" personnel during her refit. On completion was again used in similar role at Portsmouth. Finally towed from Portsmouth to Devonport on 24 April 1970 to await disposal.
4 Sept. 1972	—	Left Devonport for Cairn Ryan, where she arrived on the 8th for breaking up.

HMS Centaur (October 1953)

Light Fleet Aircraft Carriers

Notes

ALBION

May 1954	—	Completed.
1956	—	In the Mediterranean for the Suez Crisis.
July 1956	—	Carried military equipment from Portsmouth to Malta.
Jan. 1961	—	After 18 months in Far East, South African and South American waters, she was taken in hand for conversion into a Commando Carrier.
3 Nov. 1962	—	Left Portsmouth and following month was involved in the Brunei rebellion.
1963	—	Malaysian/Indonesian border troubles.
1967	—	Helped in British Withdrawal from Aden during Far East commission.
1971	—	Cold weather warfare Trials in the Arctic, then again to Far East.
22 Oct. 1973	—	Purchased for use in North Sea oilfields, left Portsmouth for the Clyde to be converted to Crane ship for service with oil rigs. New owners Wilson Watson Organisation.
16 Nov. 1973	—	Towed to Faslane for breaking up — plans to convert her having been cancelled.

HMS Albion (June 1957)

Light Fleet Aircraft Carriers

Notes

BULWARK

Oct. 1954	—	Completed.
1956	—	In the Mediterranean for the Suez crisis.
1959-60	—	Converted into Commando Carrier at Portsmouth Dockyard. Fixed wing aircraft facilities removed.
19 Jan. 1960	—	Commissioned as a Commando Carrier.
1961	—	Kuwait.
1963	—	Refit.
1964	—	Far East.
Sept. 1965-April 1966	—	Refit at Devonport Dockyard.
1970	—	Malaysia.
1972	—	HQ ship for withdrawal of British Forces from Malta.
8 March 1974	—	Arrived Devonport for refit.
1976	—	Placed in Reserve.
1977	—	Re-activated and refitted at Portsmouth as interim measure due to delays in building 'INVINCIBLE'.
23 Feb. 1979	—	Recommissioned at Portsmouth.

HMS Bulwark (January 1966)

Fleet Aircraft Carriers

AUDACIOUS CLASS

Ship	Launch Date	Builder
EAGLE (Ex-Audacious)	19 March 1946	Harland & Wolff Ltd. Belfast

Displacement 36,800 tons **Length** 803 ft. 9 ins. **Beam** 112 ft. 9 ins. **Draught** 33 ft. 3 ins. **Speed** 31.5 knots **Armament** sixteen 4.5″, fifty-eight 40mm AA, four 3 PDR **Aircraft** over 50 in peacetime **Complement** 2,300 (with Squadrons embarked).

Notes

EAGLE

1 March 1952	—	Accepted into service.
1959-64	—	Major re-construction.
14 May 1964	—	Re-commissioned for service in Far East.
1966	—	Set peacetime record of 71 days at sea — on Beira oil patrol.
6 April 1967	—	Re-commissioned.
Dec. 1971	—	Announcement that she was to be scrapped.
26 Jan. 1972	—	Arrived Portsmouth from Far East on her last voyage. There she was de-stored.
10 Aug. 1972	—	Arrived Devonport under tow.
13 Oct. 1978	—	Left Devonport for Cairn Ryan, Wigtownshire, for breaking up.

HMS Eagle (May 1955)

Fleet Aircraft Carriers

AUDACIOUS CLASS

Ship	Launch Date	Builder
ARK ROYAL (Ex-Irresistible)	3 May 1950	Cammell Laird & Co., Ltd., Birkenhead

Displacement 36,800 tons **Length** 808 ft. 3 ins. **Beam** 112 ft. 9 ins. **Draught** 33 ft. 3 ins. **Speed** 31.5 knots **Armament** sixteen 4.5″, forty-one 40mm AA, four 3 PDR. **Aircraft** over 50 in peacetime **Complement** 2,300 (with Squadrons embarked).

Notes

ARK ROYAL

22 Feb. 1955	—	First Commissioned.
1956	—	Four 4.5″ (port side forward) removed.
1959-61	—	Refit — side life removed and four 4.5″ starboard side removed. More powerful steam catapult fitted.
1964	—	Four 4.5″ either side of after sponsons removed.
1967-70	—	Modernised to operate Phantom and Buccaneer aircraft.
9 Nov. 1970	—	Collided with Russian Kotlin Class Destroyer in the Mediterranean.
1976-77	—	Last major refit.
5 April 1978	—	Sailed on last deployment.
4 Dec. 1978	—	Arrived Devonport for last time.
1979	—	Withdrawn from service.
22 Sept. 1980	—	Left Devonport for breaking up at Cairn Ryan, Wigtownshire.
28 Sept. 1980	—	Arrived Cairn Ryan.

HMS Ark Royal (July 1957)

Fleet Aircraft Carriers

HERMES CLASS [Modernised]

Ship	Launch Date	Builder
HERMES (Ex-Elephant)	16 Feb. 1953	Vickers Armstrong Ltd., Barrow-in-Furness

Displacement 23,000 tons **Length** 744 ft. 3 ins. **Beam** 144 ft. 6 ins. **Draught** 28 ft. **Speed** 28 knots **Armament** ten 40mm AA **Aircraft** twenty + eight helicopters **Complement** 2,100 (with Squadrons embarked).

Note: Originally intended as sister ship to ALBION, BULWARK and CENTAUR, but was very much modified.

Notes

HERMES

25. Nov. 1959	—	First Commissioned.
1964-66	—	Long Refit.
Mar.1971- June 1973	—	Converted to Commando Carrier when facilities for fixed wing aircraft were removed.
1976	—	Refit at Devonport, when converted to primary role as anti-submarine carrier — with Commando role retained.
1977	—	In Mediterranean.
1980/81	—	Refitted to enable her to operate Sea Harrier aircraft.

HMS Hermes (August 1966)

Fleet Aircraft Carriers

INVINCIBLE CLASS

Ship	Launch Date	Builder
INVINCIBLE	3 May 1977	Vickers (Shipbuilding Ltd) Barrow-in-Furness
ILLUSTRIOUS	1 Dec. 1978	Swan Hunter Ltd., Walls-end on-Tyne
ARK ROYAL (Ex-Indomitable)		Swan Hunter Ltd., Walls-end-on-Tyne

Displacement 16,000 tons **Length** 677 ft. **Beam** 90 ft. **Draught** 24 ft. **Speed** 28 knots **Armament** two twin "Sea Dart" **Aircraft** eighteen (ten Sea King helicopters and up to eight Sea Harriers) **Complement** 900.

Notes

INVINCIBLE

19 March 1980	—	Accepted into service at Portsmouth.
1980	—	Trials. Mediterranean & N. Atlantic.

HMS Invincible (April 1980)

Escort Aircraft Carrier

Ship	Launch Date	Builder
CAMPANIA	17 June 1943	Harland & Wolff Ltd.

Displacement 12,450 tons **Length** 540 ft. **Beam** 70 ft. **Draught** 23 ft. 6 ins. **Speed** 17 knots **Armament** two 4″, sixteen 2 PDR Pompoms, eight 40mm AA, sixteen 20mm AA **Aircraft** 20 **Complement** 700.

Notes

CAMPANIA

		Converted from the hull of a 12,000 tons refrigerated cargo vessel built for the Shaw Savill Line.
1944	—	Completed.
1948	—	To Reserve.
		Laid up in the Gareloch.
1950	—	Decided that the ship be lent for two years to the Festival of Britain (1951) Organisation as an Exhibition ship. Visited several ports.
11 Nov. 1955	—	Arrived Blyth for breaking up.

HMS Campania (June 1952)

Aircraft Maintenance Ship

Ship	Launch Date	Builder
UNICORN	20 Nov. 1941	Harland & Wolff Ltd., Belfast

Displacement 14,750 tons **Length** 640 ft. **beam** 90 ft. **Draught** 19 ft. **Speed** 24 knots **Armament** eight 4″, sixteen 2 PDR, sixteen 20mm AA **Aircraft** when operating 35 **Complement** 1,000

Notes

UNICORN

		Served as Operational Carrier during the war.
1945	—	Pacific Fleet.
1946	—	In Reserve.
1948	—	Taken out of Reserve and refitted as Maintenance and Replenishment Carrier.
1949	—	Far East.
1950-53	—	Korean War, when she operated her own aircraft and was used as an Emergency Landing Ship for aircraft from other Carriers.
1953	—	Ferry Carrier.
1955	—	Equipped for duty as Aircraft Supply and Repair ship.
15 June 1959	—	Arrived Dalmuir for breaking up. (The hull at Troon)

Aircraft Maintenance Ship

AIRCRAFT REPAIR SHIP

Ship	Launch Date	Builder
HOLM SOUND (Ex-Empire Labuan)	5 Sept. 1944	W. Gray & Co. Ltd., West Hartlepool
Displacement 10,000 tons **Length** 447 ft. **Beam** 56 ft. **Draught** 26 ft. 9 ins. **Speed** 11 knots **Armament** twelve 20mm AA.		

Notes

HOLM SOUND

Sold April 1948 — To commercial interests and re-named AVISBAY.

Aircraft Maintenance Ship

Ship	Launch Date	Builder
PERSEUS (Ex-Edgar)	26 March 1944	Vickers Armstrong, Tyne
PIONEER (Ex-Mars)	20 May 1944	Vickers Armstrong Ltd., Barrow-in-Furness.

Displacement Perseus 12,265 tons, Pioneer 12,000 tons **Length** 694 ft. 6 ins. **Beam** 80 ft. 4 ins. **Draught** 23 ft. **Speed** 25 knots **Armament** twenty-four 2 PDR, nineteen 40mm AA **Complement** 1,076.

Note: — were laid down as Colossus Class Carriers but were completed as Aircraft Maintenance Ships

PERSEUS

1947	—	In Reserve Fleet.
1949-50	—	Refitted and equipped with aircraft catapult of new design.
June 1953	—	Designated Ferry Carrier.
1955	—	Major refit and conversion at Harland & Wolff, Belfast.
1957	—	In Reserve.
6 May 1958	—	Sold to Smith and Houston for breaking up at Port Glasgow.

PIONEER

1953	—	Designated Ferry Carrier.
Sept. 1954	—	Sold to T.W. Ward for breaking up at Inverkeithing.

HMS Perseus (May 1946)

Cruisers

CAVENDISH CLASS

Ship	Launch Date	Builder
FROBISHER	20 March 1920	Devonport Dockyard

Displacement 9,860 tons **Length** 605 ft. **Beam** 65 ft. (across bulges) **Draught** 17 ft. 3 ins. **Speed** 30.5 knots **Armament** five 7.5″. five 4″ AA, sixteen 2 PDR AA, seven 20mm AA **Torpedo Tubes** four 21″ (fixed) **Complement** 712.

Notes

FROBISHER

1945	—	Became Cadets' Training Ship.
April 1947	—	Relieved by DEVONSHIRE and placed in Reserve in Devonport.
26 March 1949	—	Sold to British Iron and Steel Corporation.
11 May 1949	—	Arrived Newport for breaking up.

HMS Frobisher (January 1946)

Cruisers

KENT CLASS

Ship	Launch Date	Builder
CUMBERLAND	16 March 1926	Vickers Ltd. Barrow.

Displacement 10,800 tons **Length** 630 ft. **Beam** 68 ft. 3 ins. (across bulges) **Draught** 16 ft. 3 ins. **Speed** 31.5 knots **Armament** eight 8″, eight 4″ AA, eight 2 PDR AA, eight 0.5″ AA **Torpedo Tubes** eight 21″ (quadrupled) **Complement** 685.

Notes

CUMBERLAND

1949-51	—	Converted to Navy's first Trials Cruiser with reduced armament. Tested everything from guided missiles to plastic covered tables. Every few months, ship refitted at Devonport.
14 Jan. 1959	—	Paid off.
3 Nov. 1959	—	Arrived Newport for breaking up.

HMS Cumberland (November 1958)

Cruisers

LONDON CLASS (1st GROUP)

Ship	Launch Date	Builder
DEVONSHIRE	22 Oct. 1927	Devonport Dockyard
SUSSEX	22 Feb. 1928	Hawthorn Leslie, Hebburn-on-Tyne

Displacement 9,850 tons **Length** 633 ft. **Beam** 66 ft. **Draught** 17 ft. **Speed** 32.25 knots **Armament** six 8″, eight 4″ AA, thirty-two 2 PDR AA, twenty-eight 20mm AA **Torpedo Tubes** eight 21″ (Quadrupled) **Complement** 700.

Notes

DEVONSHIRE

April 1947	—	Replaced "FROBISHER" as Cadet Training Ship.
Feb. 1951	—	Landed armed Parties in Grenada.
1953	—	Oldest warship present at the Coronation Review.
16 June 1954	—	Sold to J. Cashmore Ltd.
10 Dec. 1954	—	Left Devonport for Newport, Mon., for breaking up.

SUSSEX

1947-48	—	Flag Officer Commanding 5th Cruiser Squadron and Second-in-Command Far East.
3 Jan. 1950	—	Sold to Arnott Young.
23 Feb. 1950	—	Arrived Dalmuir for breaking up.

HMS Devonshire (July 1949)

Cruisers

LONDON CLASS (2nd GROUP)

Ship	Launch Date	Builder
LONDON	14 Sept. 1927	Portsmouth Dockyard

Displacement 10,500 tons **Length** 633 ft. **Beam** 66 ft. **Draught** 17 ft. **Speed** 32.25 knots **Armament** eight 8″, eight 4″ AA, sixteen 2 PDR AA, four 40mm AA, twenty 20mm AA, eight 0.5″ AA **Torpedo Tubes** eight 21″ (quadrupled) **Complement** 789.

Notes

LONDON

1946	—	Flag Officer Commanding, Reserve Fleet.
1948	—	Commander-in-Chief, Far East.
3 Jan. 1950	—	Sold to T.W. Ward.
22 Jan. 1950	—	Arrived Barrow for breaking up.

DORSETSHIRE CLASS

Ship	Launch Date	Builder
NORFOLK	12 Dec. 1928	Fairfield Shipbuilding & Eng. Co., Govan.

Displacement 9,925 tons **Length** 630 ft. **Beam** 66 ft. **Draught** 17 ft. **Speed** 32.25 knots **Armament** six 8″, eight 4″ AA, sixteen 2 PDR AA, four 40mm AA, eight 0.5″ AA **Complement** 710.

June-Sept.1945	—	Refitted at Devonport.
Dec.1945-47	—	Flagship of Commander-in-Chief, East Indies.
Oct. 1946-May 1947	—	Refitted at Simonstown.
3 May 1949	—	Arrived Devonport for reduction to Reserve.
3 Nov. 1949	—	Towed to Falmouth for laying up.
19 Feb. 1950	—	Arrived Newport for breaking up.

HMS London (September 1947)

Cruisers

LEANDER CLASS — FIRST GROUP

Ship	Launch Date	Builder
LEANDER	24 Sept. 1931	Devonport Dockyard

Displacement 7,270 tons **Length** 554 ft. 3 ins. **Beam** 55 ft. 9 ins **Draught** 16 ft. **Speed** 32.5 knots **Armament** six 6″, eight 4″ AA, seven 40mm AA, four 20mm AA **Torpedo Tubes** eight 21″ (quadrupled) **Complement** 570.

Notes

LEANDER

1945	—	Whilst undergoing 2 year refit (War damage) in the U.S.A., work was suspended and ship brought home to complete the job on the Tyne.
1947	—	First Cruiser Squadron in the Mediterranean. Paid off at Chatham and afterwards returned to Devonport. Was then laid up at Falmouth before being brought forward for ship target trials.
15 Dec. 1949	—	Sold to Hughes Bolckow.
15 Jan. 1950	—	Arrived Blyth for breaking up.

Another ship of this class, ACHILLES, was loaned to R.N.Z.N. (1936-1943) and then sold to the Royal Indian Navy in 1948 and renamed DELHI.

HMS Leander (July 1946)

Cruisers

LEANDER CLASS — FIRST GROUP

Ship	Launch Date	Builder
ORION	24 Nov. 1932	Devonport Dockyard
AJAX	1 March 1934	Vickers Armstrong Ltd., Barrow-in-Furness

Displacement 7,215 tons (Ajax — 6,950 tons) **Length** 554 ft. 3 ins. **Beam** 55 ft. 9 ins. **Draught** 16 ft. **Speed** 32.5 knots **Armament** eight 6″, eight 4″ AA, eight 2 PDR AA, seven 20mm AA (Ajax 13) **Torpedo Tubes** eight 21″ (quadrupled) **Complement** 570.

Notes

ORION

5 July 1946	—	Returned to Devonport for refit, after two years in the Mediterranean.
1948	—	Underwater explosion Trials in Loch Striven in Scotland.
19 July 1949	—	Sold to the West of Scotland Shipbreaking Company.
Aug. 1949	—	Arrived Troon for breaking up.

AJAX

Aug. 1945	—	Flagship of Commander-in-Chief, Mediterranean.
Sept. 1945 -Jan. 1946	—	Refitted at Malta.
1946-48	—	First Cruiser Squadron in the Mediterranean.
16 Feb. 1948	—	Arrived Chatham to reduce to Reserve.
Summer 1948	—	Laid up at Falmouth.
1949	—	Sold to J. Cashmore Ltd.
13 Nov. 1949	—	Arrived Newport for breaking up.

HMS Ajax (January 1938)

Cruisers

ARETHUSA CLASS — FIRST GROUP

Ship	Launch Date	Builder
ARETHUSA	6 March 1934	Chatham Dockyard

Displacement 5,900 tons (about 700 tons having been added during war-time modifications) **Length** 506 ft. **Beam** 51 ft. **Draught** 14 ft. **Speed** 32.25 knots **Armament** six 6″, eight 4″ AA, eight 40mm AA, eight 0.5″ AA **Torpedo Tubes** six 21″ (tripled) **Complement** 500.

Notes

ARETHUSA

1945	—	Mediterranean Fleet.
Oct. 1945	—	Paid off into Reserve at Chatham.
Jan. 1948	—	Laid up at Falmouth.
Aug. 1948	—	Approved for use as a target.
1950	—	Sold to J. Cashmore Ltd.
9 May 1950	—	Arrived Newport for breaking up.

Ship	Launch Date	Builder
AURORA	20 Aug. 1936	Portsmouth Dockyard

Displacement 5,270 tons **Length** 506 ft. **Beam** 51 ft. **Draught** 14 ft. **Speed** 32.25 knots **Armament** six 6″, eight 4″ AA, six 20mm AA, eight 0.5″ AA **Torpedo Tubes** six 21″ (tripled) **Complement** 500.

1945	—	Mediterranean Fleet.
17 April 1946	—	Arrived Portsmouth to pay off into Reserve.
Feb. 1947	—	Refit, pending transfer to China.
1948	—	Sold to Nationalist Chinese Navy and re-named TCHOUNGKING.
March 1949	—	Bombed and sunk in Taku Harbour.
1951	—	Salvaged and re-named HSUANG HO.
1951	—	Again re-named PEI CHING; and then KUANG CHOU.
1955	—	Hulked.

HMS Arethusa (June 1935)

HMS Aurora (April 1946)

Cruisers

SOUTHAMPTON CLASS — FIRST GROUP

Ship	Launch Date	Builder
NEWCASTLE (Ex-Minotaur)	23 Jan. 1936	Vickers Armstrong, Tyne
GLASGOW	20 June 1936	Scotts Shipbuilding & Eng. Co., Ltd. Greenock
SHEFFIELD	23 July 1936	Vickers Armstrong, Tyne
BIRMINGHAM	2 Sept. 1936	Devonport Dockyard

Displacement 9,100 tons **Length** 591 ft. 6 ins. **Beam** 61 ft. 8 ins **Draught** 17 ft. **Speed** 32 knots **Armament** nine 6″ (X turret. removed in 1945), eight 4″ AA, sixteen 2 PDR AA, eighteen 20mm AA **Torpedo Tubes** six 21″ (tripled) **Complement** 750.

Notes

NEWCASTLE

Oct. 1945	—	Refitting at Rosyth.
Nov. 1945	—	Trooping Duties.
Sept. 1946-Aug. 1947	—	Refitting at Devonport, then to the Mediterranean.
1948	—	Flagship of First Cruiser Squadron.
Feb. 1950-May 1952	—	Reconstructed at Devonport.
1952	—	Far East Station (inc. Korea).
Oct. 1953	—	Flagship of 5th Cruiser Squadron in Far East.
Nov. 1955	—	Re-commissioned at Singapore. Ship's Companies were exchanged by air, the first ship in R.N. to do so.
Dec. 1957	—	Flagship of Commander-in-Chief, Far East.
Aug. 1958	—	Arrived Portsmouth.
19 Aug. 1959	—	Arrived Faslane for breaking up.

HMS Newcastle (June 1954)

Cruisers

Notes

SHEFFIELD

Details as for NEWCASTLE except fitted — eight 2 PDR., sixteen 40mm AA, & eleven 20mm AA.

1947-48	—	Flagship of Commander-in-Chief, America and West Indies.
1949-51	—	Long Refit.
1951	—	Flagship of Commander-in-Chief, America and West Indies.
1952	—	Flagship of Flag Officer, Heavy Squadron, Home Fleet.
1953	—	Flagship of Commander-in-Chief, America and West Indies.
1956-57	—	Refit.
1959-60	—	Refitted and into operational Reserve, Portsmouth. Headquarters of Commodore Reserve Ships.
Sept. 1967	—	Arrived Faslane for breaking up.

HMS Sheffield (June 1946)

Cruisers

Notes

GLASGOW — details as for Newcastle except fitted — twenty-six 2 PDR, seventeen 20mm AA.

Sept. 1945	—	Flagship of 5th Cruiser Squadron in East Indies.
Sept. 1946	—	Flagship of 4th Cruiser Squadron in East Indies.
1948	—	Refit at Portsmouth.
1950	—	West Indies.
April 1951	—	Refitted at Chatham.
1952	—	Flagship of Commander-in-Chief, Mediterranean.
1953	—	Flagship of Commander-in-Chief, Mediterranean, at the Coronation Review at Spithead.
May 1955	—	Flagship of Flag Officer Flotillas Home Fleet.
Nov. 1956	—	Reduced to Reserve Fleet at Portsmouth.
March 1958	—	At Portsmouth for disposal.
8 July 1958	—	Arrived Blyth for breaking up

BIRMINGHAM — details as for Newcastle except fitted — eight 2 2PDR, sixteen 40mm AA, twelve 20mm AA.

May 1945	—	In Copenhagen for surrender of German Forces.
1948-49	—	Flagship of Commander-in-Chief, East Indies.
1950-52	—	Extensively modernised and re-constructed at Portsmouth.
1953	—	Korean War.
1955	—	Flagship of Flag Officer, Second-in-Command, Far East.
1956	—	In Mediterranean.
Dec. 1959	—	Placed in Reserve in Devonport.
1960	—	Sold to T.W. Ward.
2 Sept. 1960	—	Left Devonport for breaking up at Inverkeithing.

HMS Birmingham (June 1952)

Cruisers

SOUTHAMPTON CLASS — SECOND GROUP

Ship	Launch Date	Builder
LIVERPOOL	24 March 1937	Fairfield Shipbuilding & Eng. Co., Ltd., Govan.

Displacement 9,400 tons **Length** 591 ft. 6 ins. **Beam** 62 ft. 3 ins **Draught** 17 ft. 6 ins. **Speed** 32 knots **Armament** nine 6", eight 4" AA, twenty-eight 2 PDR AA **Aircraft** two aircraft and a catapult **Torpedo Tubes** six 21" (tripled) **Complement** 800.

Notes

LIVERPOOL

1942	—	Was heavily damaged and did not see any further war service.
1949-50	—	Flagship of First Cruiser Squadron & Flag Officer Second-in-Command Mediterranean, who at the time was Rear Admiral The Earl Mountbatten of Burma.
1953	—	Paid off into Reserve.
2 July 1958	—	Arrived Bo'ness for breaking up.

HMS Liverpool (April 1948)

Cruisers

SOUTHAMPTON CLASS — THIRD GROUP

Ship	Launch Date	Builder
BELFAST	17 March 1938	Harland & Wolff Ltd., Belfast.

Displacement 10,565 tons (includes additions after 1939-42 refit) **Length** 613 ft. 6 ins. **Beam** 68 ft. (includes about four feet added when bulges were fitted 1939-42) **Speed** 32.25 knots **Armament** twelve 6″, eight 4″ AA, thirty-four 2 PDR AA, eighteen 20mm AA **Torpedo Tubes** six 21″ (tripled) - removed during 1955-59 refit **Complement** 850.

Notes

BELFAST

1945-50	—	In Far East.
1951-52	—	Korean War.
1952	—	Flagship of Flag Officer, 5th Cruiser Squadron and Second-in-Command Far East Station.
1955-59	—	Reconstructed at Devonport.
12 May 1959	—	Re-commissioned at Devonport for Far East Fleet.
1960	—	Flagship of Flag Officer Cruiser Squadron and Flag Officer Second-in-Command Far East, until 1962.
19 June 1962	—	Arrived Portsmouth and re-commissioned as Flagship of Flag Officer Flotillas, Home Fleet.
1963	—	Refitted at Devonport, but afterwards placed in Reserve.
Aug. 1965	—	Removed from Reserve and used as Accommodation ship at Portsmouth.
1971	—	Preserved by H.M.S. BELFAST Trust in the Pool of London.

HMS Belfast (October 1947)

Cruisers

DIDO CLASS — FIRST GROUP

Ship	Launch Date	Builder
PHOEBE	25 March 1939	Fairfield Shipbuilding & Eng. Co. Ltd. Govan
EURYALUS	6 June 1939	Chatham Dockyard
DIDO	18 July 1939	Cammell Laird & Co., Ltd., Birkenhead
CLEOPATRA	27 March 1940	R. & W. Hawthorn Leslie & Co. Hebburn-on-Tyne
SCYLLA	24 July 1940	Scotts Shipbuilding & Eng. Co. Ltd. Greenock
SIRIUS	18 Sept. 1940	Portsmouth Dockyard
ARGONAUT	6 Sept. 1941	Cammell Laird & Co. Birkenhead.

Displacement 5,600 tons **Length** 512 ft. **Beam** 50 ft. 6 ins.
Draught 14 ft. **Speed** 33 knots **Armament** ten 5.25", eight 2
PDR AA, twelve 20mm AA **Torpedo Tubes** six 21" (tripled)
Complement 480.

Notes

DIDO

Oct. 1947	—	To Reserve Fleet.
1952	—	Flagship of Flag Officer, Commanding Reserve Fleet.
1955	—	In Reserve.
16 July 1957	—	Arrived Barrow for breaking up.

EURYALUS

1946	—	In Reserve.
1948	—	In the Mediterranean.
March 1953	—	Left Mediterranean for South Atlantic.
Aug. 1954	—	Paid off at Devonport.
18 July 1959	—	Arrived Blyth for breaking up.

HMS Euryalus (February 1947)

Cruisers

Notes

PHEOBE — details as over except **Armament** eight 5.25″, twelve 40mm AA, sixteen 20 mm AA.

1946-47	—	Flagship of Mediterranean Fleet Destroyers, and then First Cruiser Squadron.
1952	—	In Reserve.
1 Aug. 1956	—	Arrived Blyth for breaking up.

CLEOPATRA — details as Phoebe (except fourteen 20mm AA.)

1945	—	Home Fleet.
1953	—	In Reserve.
1954-56	—	Flagship of Flag Officer Commanding Reserve Fleet.
15 Dec. 1958	—	Arrived Newport for breaking up.

SCYLLA — details as Phoebe (except twelve 40mm AA, eight 20 mm AA.)

1948	—	On disposal list on account of heavy underwater damage during the war. Used for ship target trials.
6 May 1950	—	Arrived Barrow for breaking up.

SIRIUS — details as Phoebe (except eight 2 PDR AA, five 40mm AA.)

May 1947	—	Returned from the Mediterranean to join the 2nd Cruiser Squadron, Home Fleet.
1949	—	To Reserve.
15 Oct. 1956	—	Arrived Blyth for breaking up.

ARGONAUT — details as Phoebe (except twelve 2 PDR AA, five 40mm AA, two 20mm AA.)

1946	—	In Reserve Fleet.
19 Nov. 1955	—	Arrived Newport for breaking up.

HMS Dido (June 1953)

Cruisers

DIDO CLASS — SECOND GROUP

Ship	Launch Date	Builder
ROYALIST	30 May 1942	Scotts Shipbuilding & Eng. Co. Ltd., Greenock
DIADEM	26 Aug. 1942	R`& W Hawthorn Leslie & Co., Hebburn-on-Tyne
BLACK PRINCE	27 Aug. 1942	Harland & Wolff, Belfast
BELLONA	29 Sept. 1942	Fairfield Shipbuilding & Eng. Co. Ltd., Govan.

Displacement 5,950 tons **Length** 512 ft. **Beam** 50 ft. 6 ins. **Draught** 15 ft. **Speed** 33 knots **Armament** eight 5.25″, twelve 2 PDR AA, twelve 20mm AA **Torpedo Tubes** six 21″ (tripled) **Complement** 530.

Notes

ROYALIST

1947	—	Reserve Fleet.
1955	—	Re-constructed.
1956-57	—	Transferred to Royal New Zealand Navy.
1967	—	Returned to R.N.
Jan. 1968	—	Arrived Osaka in Japan for breaking up.

DIADEM

1948	—	Flagship of 2nd Cruiser Squadron.
1950	—	To Reserve.
1956	—	Transferred to Pakistan Navy and re-named BABUR.

BLACK PRINCE

1948-62	—	Loaned to R.N.Z.N.
2 March 1962		Arrived in Japan for breaking up

BELLONA

1948-56	—	Loaned to R.N.Z.N.
5 Feb. 1959	—	Arrived Briton Ferry for breaking up.

HMS Black Prince (May 1953)

Cruisers

FIJI CLASS

Ship	Launch Date	Builder
NIGERIA	18 July 1939	Vickers Armstrong Ltd. Tyne
MAURITIUS	19 July 1939	Swan Hunter & Wigham Richardson. Wallsend
KENYA	18 Aug. 1939	Alex. Stephen & Son, Ltd. Govan
JAMAICA	16 Nov. 1940	Vickers Armstrong Ltd. Barrow-in-Furness.
GAMBIA	30 Nov. 1940	Swan Hunter & Wigham Richardson, Wallsend
BERMUDA	11 Sept. 1941	John Brown & Co. Ltd. Clydebank.

Displacement 9,200 tons **Length** 555 ft. 6 ins. **Beam** 62 ft. **Draught** 17 ft. 6ins. **Speed** 33 knots **Armament** (Kenya) nine 6″, eight 4″ AA, eighteen 40mm; (Mauritius) nine 6″, eight 4″ AA, twenty 2 PDR, twenty 20mm; (Jamaica) nine 6″, eight 4″ AA, twenty 2 PDR, eighteen 20mm; (Bermuda) nine 6″, eight 4″ AA, twenty 2 PDR, four 40mm, eight 20mm; (Nigeria & Gambia) twelve 6″, eight 4″ AA, eight 2 PDR, eighteen 20mm. **Torpedo Tubes** six 21″ (tripled) **Complement** 730.

Notes

NIGERIA

1946-50	—	Flagship of Commander-in-Chief, South Atlantic.
1951	—	Paid Off.
April 1954	—	Purchased by Royal Indian Navy and renamed MYSORE (29 Aug. 1957).
1956-57	—	Extensive refit.
1975	—	In service as Training Ship.

HMS Kenya (October 1946)

Cruisers

MAURITIUS

1946	—	Flagship of 15th Cruiser Squadron.
1946-47	—	Flagship of First Cruiser Squadron.
1950-51	—	Flagship of Commander-in-Chief, E. Indies.
1952	—	Paid off.
27 March 1965	—	Arrived Inverkeithing for breaking up.

KENYA

1945	—	Returned home from Far East, then served on America and West Indies Station.
1950	—	Relieved LONDON in the Far East.
1951-52	—	Flagship of Commander-in-Chief, E.Indies
1953-55	—	Long Refit.
1956	—	Flagship of Commander-in-Chief, America and West Indies Station.
29 Oct. 1962	—	Arrived Faslane for breaking up.

JAMAICA

1946-52	—	In Commission.
1953	—	Flag Officer Commander Reserve Fleet.
1954-55	—	In Commission.
1958	—	In Reserve.
20 Dec. 1960	—	Arrived Dalmuir for stripping, hull moved to Troon for breaking up in 1962.

GAMBIA

1943-47	—	Royal New Zealand Navy.
1948	—	Returned to R.N.
1951	—	Flagship of Flag Officer Second-in-Command, Mediterranean and First Cruiser Squadron.
1956-58	—	Flagship of Commander-in-Chief, E.Indies
1960	—	In Reserve.
5 Dec. 1968	—	Arrived Inverkeithing for breaking up.

BERMUDA

1946	—	Flagship of 5th Cruiser Squadron.
1951-52	—	Flagship of Commander-in-Chief, S. Atlantic.
1955-56	—	Flagship of Flag Officer Flotillas, Home Fleet —again in 1962.
1963	—	Paid off into Reserve.
26 Aug. 1965	—	Arrived Briton Ferry for breaking up.

HMS Bermuda (March 1958)

Cruisers

FIJI CLASS — MODIFIED DESIGN

Ship	Launch Date	Builder
UGANDA	7 Aug. 1941	V. Armstrong Ltd., Tyne
NEWFOUNDLAND	19 Dec. 1941	Swan Hunter & Wigham Richardson, Wallsend
CEYLON	30 July 1942	A. Stephen & Sons, Govan

Displacement 9,200 tons (including wartime additions) **Length** 555 ft. 6 ins. **Beam** 62 ft. **Draught** 17 ft. 6 ins. **Speed** 33 knots **Armament** nine 6″, eight 4″ AA, sixteen 2 PDR AA, twenty 20mm AA (Uganda — Eight PDR.AA, eight 40mm AA, sixteen 20mm AA) **Torpedo Tubes** six 21″ (tripled) **Complement** 730.

Notes

UGANDA

1944	—	Transferred to the Royal Canadian Navy and re-named QUEBEC. Employed as Training Cruiser on East Coast of Canada.
6 Feb. 1961	—	Arrived Osaka for breaking up.

NEWFOUNDLAND

1946	—	Flagship of 5th Cruiser Squadron.
1948-50	—	Attached to H.M.S. Raleigh as Harbour Training Ship for Engine Room personnel.
1956	—	Flagship of 5th Cruiser Squadron and Flag Officer Second-in-Command Far East.
30 Dec. 1959	—	Transferred to the Peruvian Navy at Portsmouth and re-named ALMIRANTE GRAU.

CEYLON

1955-56	—	Refitted.
1958	—	Flagship - Flag Officer Flotillas, Home Fleet.
9 Feb. 1960	—	Transferred to the Peruvian Navy at Portsmouth. Re-named CORONEL BOLOGNESI.

HMS Ceylon (September 1956)

Cruisers

MINOTAUR CLASS — FIRST GROUP

Ship	Launch Date	Builder
SWIFTSURE	4 Feb. 1943	Vickers-Armstrong, Tyne
MINOTAUR	29 July 1943	Harland & Wolff Ltd, Belfast

Displacement 8,800 tons **Length** 555 ft. 6 ins. **Beam** 63 ft. **Draught** 17 ft. 3 ins. **Speed** 32.5 knots **Armament** nine 6″, ten 4″ AA, sixteen 2 PDR AA, six 40mm AA **Torpedo Tubes** six 21″ (tripled) **Complement** 855.

Notes

SWIFTSURE

1946	—	Flagship of 4th Cruiser Squadron.
1951	—	Flagship of 2nd Cruiser Squadron.
1953	—	Flagship of Flag Officer Flotillas Home Fleet.
1955	—	Paid Off.
1957	—	In Reserve.
17 Oct. 1962	—	Arrived Inverkeithing for breaking up.

MINOTAUR

1945	—	Manned by Royal Canadian Navy and renamed ONTARIO.
1950	—	Refitted, then employed as Training Cruiser on Canada's West Coast.
19 Nov. 1960	—	Arrived Osaka in Japan for breaking up.

HMS Swiftsure (August 1946)

Cruisers

MINOTAUR CLASS — SECOND GROUP

Ship	Launch Date	Builder
SUPERB	31 Aug. 1943	Swan Hunter & Wigham Richardson, Wallsend

Displacement 8,885 tons   **Length** 555 ft. 6 ins.   **Beam** 64 ft. **Draught** 17 ft. 3 ins.   **Speed** 32.5 knots   **Armament** nine 6″, ten 4″ AA, sixteen 2 PDR AA, six 40mm AA   **Torpedo Tubes** six 21″ (tripled)   **Complement** 867.

"SUPERB" was the only ship of this group to be completed by the end of the war. Others, when eventually completed, formed the "TIGER" Class.

Notes

SUPERB

1946-47 & 1949-50	—	Flagship of 2nd Cruiser Squadron.
1951	—	Commander-in-Chief American and West Indies Station.
1952	—	Flagship of Flag′ Officer Flotillas, Home Fleet.
1953	—	Commander-in-Chief American and West Indies Station.
1954	—	Flagship of Flag Officer Flotillas, Home Fleet.
1955	—	Commander-in-Chief, America and West Indies Station.
1957	—	Commander-in-Chief, East Indies Station.
1958	—	In Reserve.
8 Aug. 1960	—	Arrived Dalmuir for stripping — the hull being broken up at Troon.

HMS Superb (September 1949)

Cruisers

TIGER CLASS

Ship	Launch Date	Builder
BLAKE (Ex-Tiger)	20 Dec. 1945	Fairfield Shipbuilding & Eng. Co. Ltd. Govan
LION (Ex-Defence)	2 Sept. 1944	Scotts Shipbuilding & Eng. Co. Ltd. Greenock (To Launching Stage)
TIGER (Ex-Blake, Ex-Bellerophon)	25 Oct. 1945	John Brown & Co. Ltd. Clydebank

Displacement 9,630 tons **Length** 555 ft. 6 ins. **Beam** 64 ft. **Draught** 18 ft. **Speed** 31.5 knots **Armament** four 6″, six 3″ **Complement** 716.

Note:— These ships were laid down and launched as a Second Group of the "MINOTAUR" Class. However, when work recommenced in 1954 it was to a revised design to form the "TIGER" Class.

Notes

TIGER

July 1946	—	Work stopped.
15 Oct. 1954	—	Decision to proceed to completion was announced.
March 1959	—	First Commissioned.
1962-63	—	In Far East.
1966	—	Used as floating conference centre for Rhodesian talks between Mr. Harold Wilson and Mr. Ian Smith.
1968-72	—	Converted at Devonport to Command Helicopter Cruiser.
7 July 1972	—	Recommissioned.
1978	—	Flagship — Flag Officer, Second Flotilla.
20 April 1978	—	Arrived Portsmouth, and paid off into Reserve. For disposal.

HMS Tiger (March 1959)

Cruisers

Notes

LION

July 1946	—	Work stopped.
15 Oct. 1954	—	Decision to proceed to completion was announced. Completed by Swan, Hunter & Wigham Richardson, Wallsend-on-Tyne.
1963-64	—	Flagship of Flag Officer Flotillas, Home Fleet.
1972	—	Approved for scrapping.
15 May 1973	—	Berthed at Rosyth to be stripped of re-usable equipment.
24 Feb. 1975	—	Arrived Inverkeithing for breaking up.

BLAKE

July 1946	—	Work stopped.
15 Oct. 1954	—	Decision to proceed to completion was announced.
Jan. 1961	—	First Commissioned.
1964	—	In Reserve.
1965-69	—	Converted at Portsmouth into Command Helicopter Cruiser.
21 Nov. 1968	—	Commenced Trials.
23 April 1969	—	Commissioned.
1969-70	—	Flagship of Flag Officer Flotillas, Western Fleet.
23 Feb. 1970	—	Left Portsmouth on 8 months round the world trip.
1974-79	—	Flagship of First Flotilla.
6 Dec. 1979	—	Arrived Portsmouth to pay off.
13 May 1980	—	Arrived Chatham, after refit at Rosyth, for Reserve Fleet.

HMS Blake (May 1969)

Monitors

Ship	Launch Date	Builder
ROBERTS	1 Feb. 1941	John Brown & Co. Ltd., Clydebank
ABERCROMBIE	31 March 1942	Vickers Armstrong Ltd., Tyne

Displacement Abercrombie 7,850 tons, Roberts 7,970 tons **Length** 373 ft. 4 ins. **Beam** 89 ft. 9 ins. **Draught** 11 ft. **Speed** 12 knots **Armament** two 15″, eight 4″, twelve 2 PDR AA, twenty 20mm AA **Complement** 350.

Note: These ships were armed with the 15″ guns formerly mounted in MARSHAL SOULT and other discarded monitors.

Notes

ROBERTS

22 Nov. 1945	—	Returned to Devonport from Far East. Used as a Turret Drill Ship; then Accommodation Ship for Reserve Fleet in Devonport until 1963.
1963	—	Placed in Reserve in the Hamoaze.
19 July 1965	—	Left Devonport for breaking up at Inverkeithing.

ABERCROMBIE

6 Nov. 1945	—	Returned to Sheerness from Far East. Used as an Accommodation ship.
July 1946	—	Replaced EREBUS as a Turret Drill ship at Chatham.
1949	—	Living ship for Nore Command Reserve Fleet.
1953	—	Towed to Portsmouth to be laid up in Fareham Creek.
17 Dec. 1954	—	Towed from Portsmouth for breaking up at Barrow.

HMS Abercrombie (July 1947)

Part 2 of this book will cover Submarines, Depot and Repair Ships. If you wish to be advised of it's publication date — write to the publishers — Maritime Books, Duloe, Liskeard, Cornwall PL14 4PE.